MY CUPCAKES COLORING BOOK

ILLUSTRATIONS BY
LYNNETTE EWOLDT JONES

DEDICATION

For my daughters, Homiya and Thamarai
Love Always,
Mom.

ISBN: 9781533185969

Live everyday
as if it is
your Birthday !

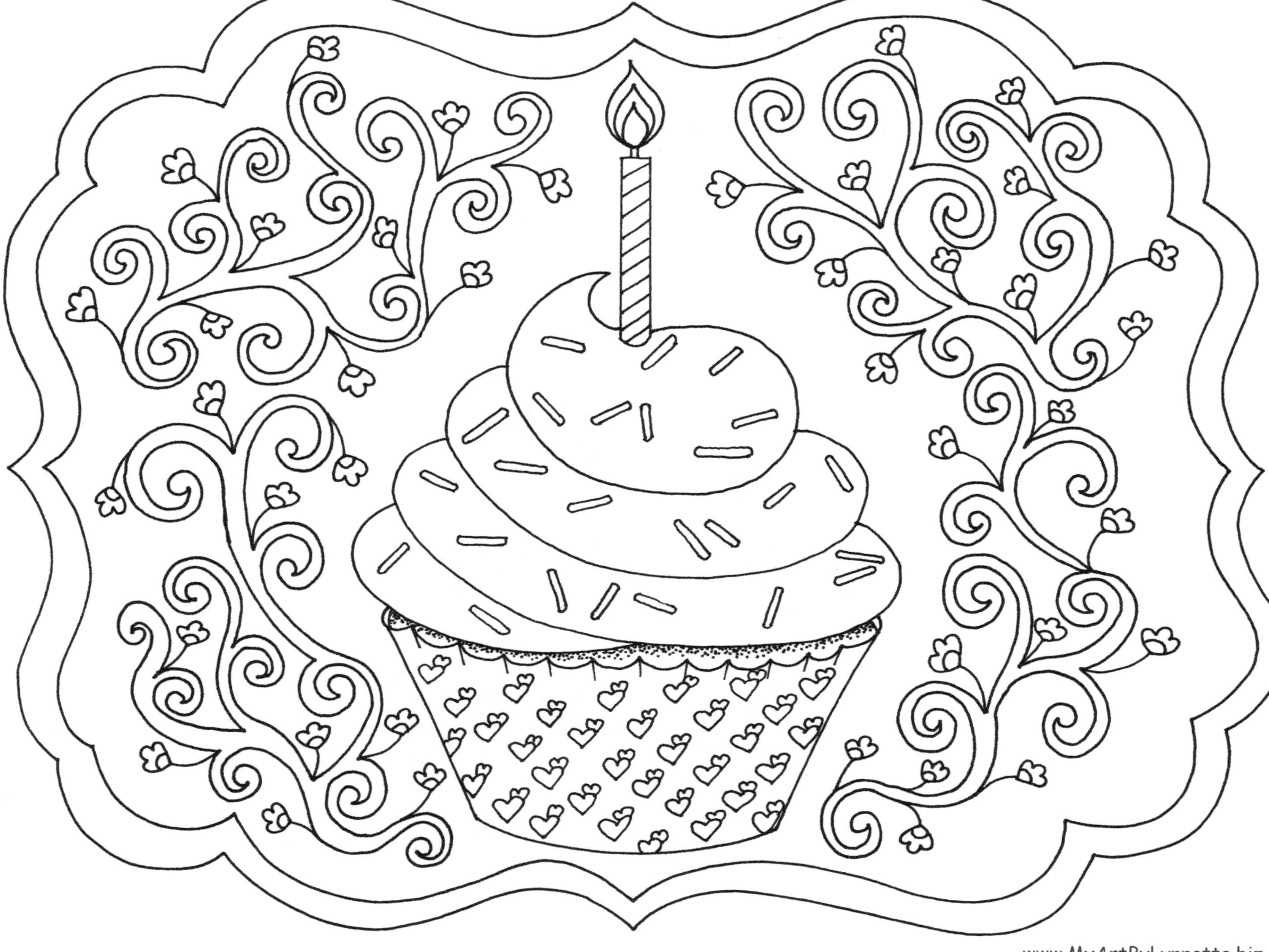

I want to have

my Cupcake

and eat it

TOO!

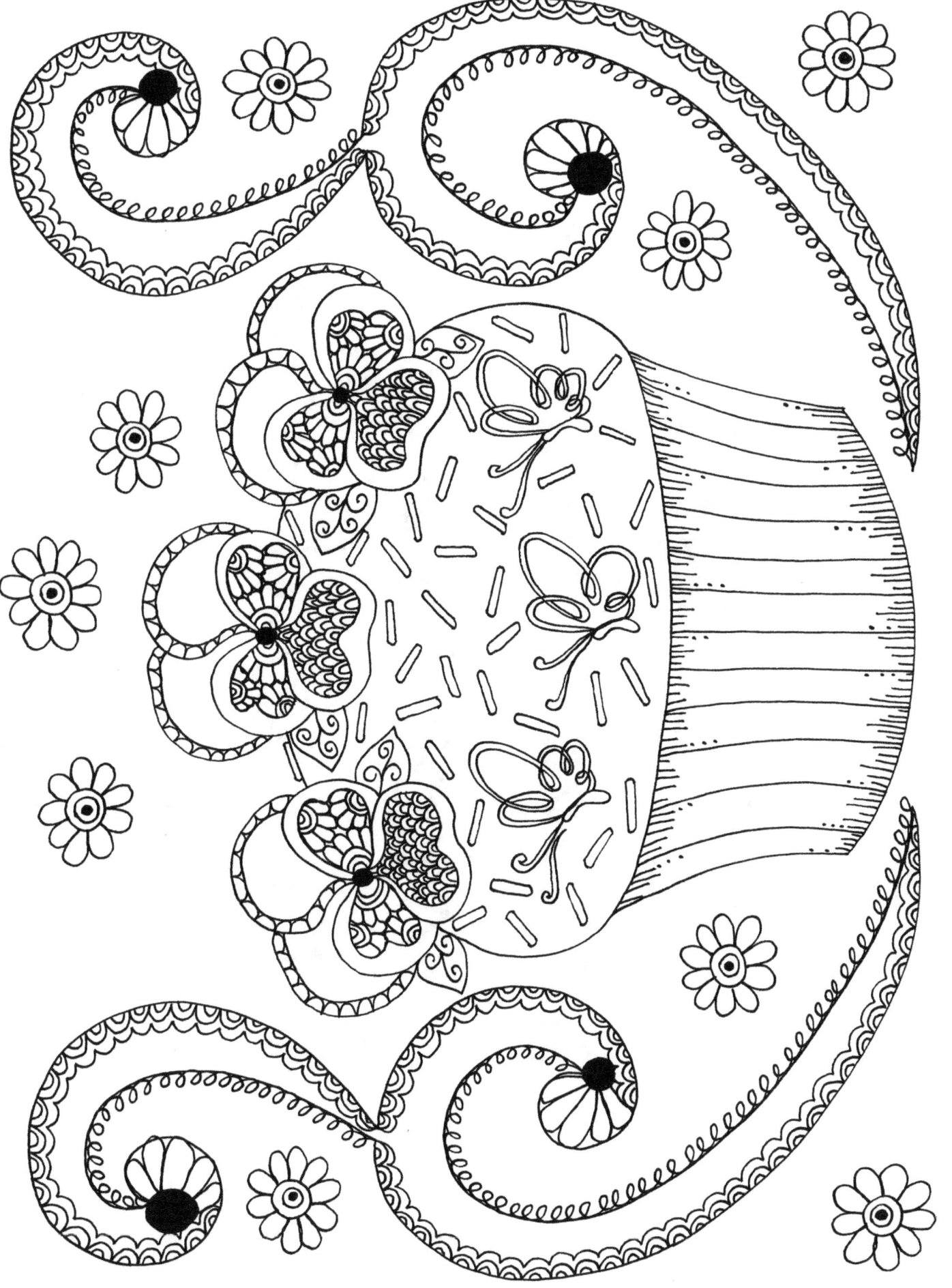

Cupcakes
are even sweeter
when shared
with a good friend.

www.MyArtByLynnette.biz

I want to eat Cupcakes

by the Ocean

with You!

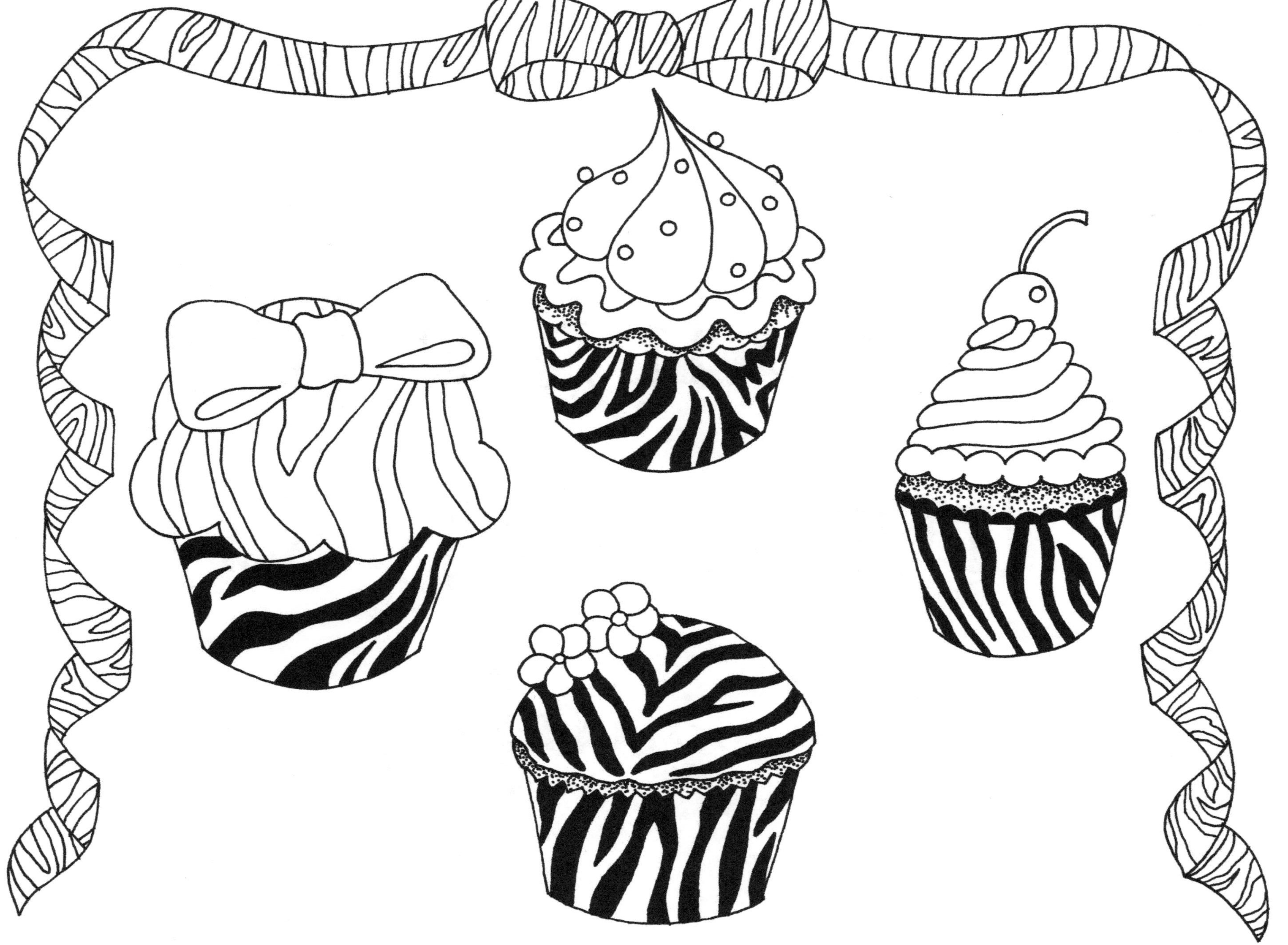

www.MyArtByLynnette.biz

Before you
try, try again...
Eat a Cupcake!

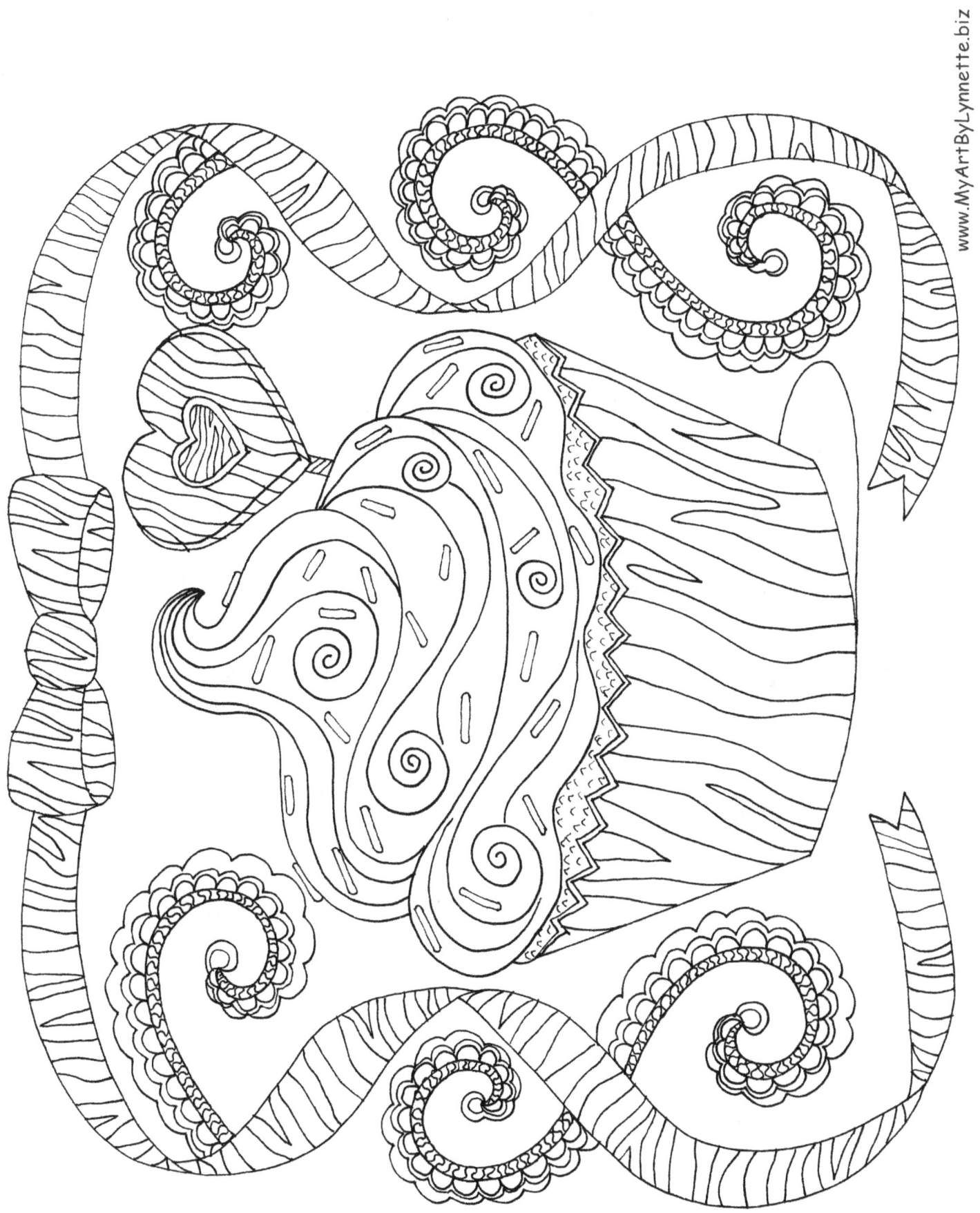

KEEP CALM & EAT A CUPCAKE

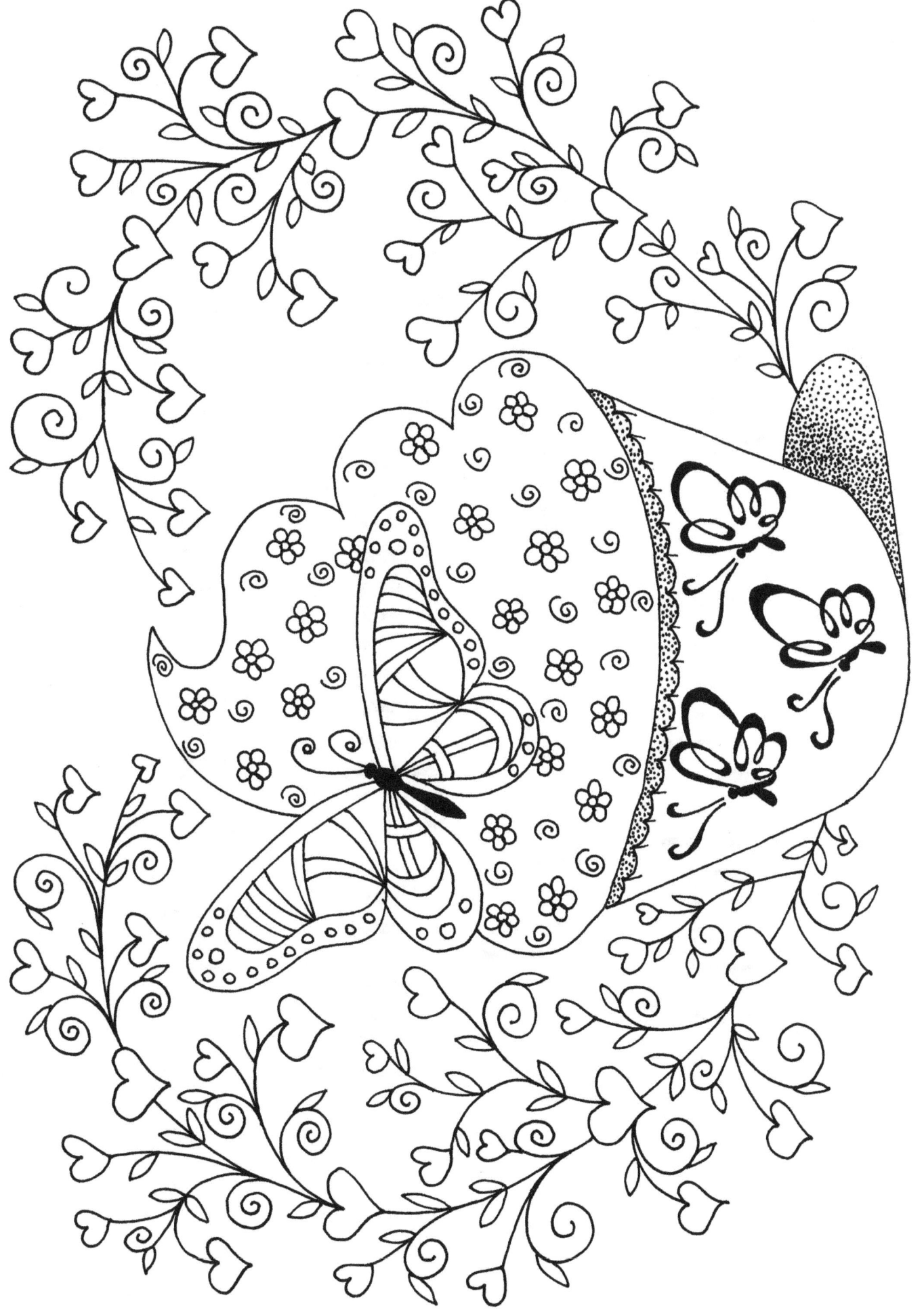

May your Heart
be full of Love and
your Tummy full
of Cupcakes!

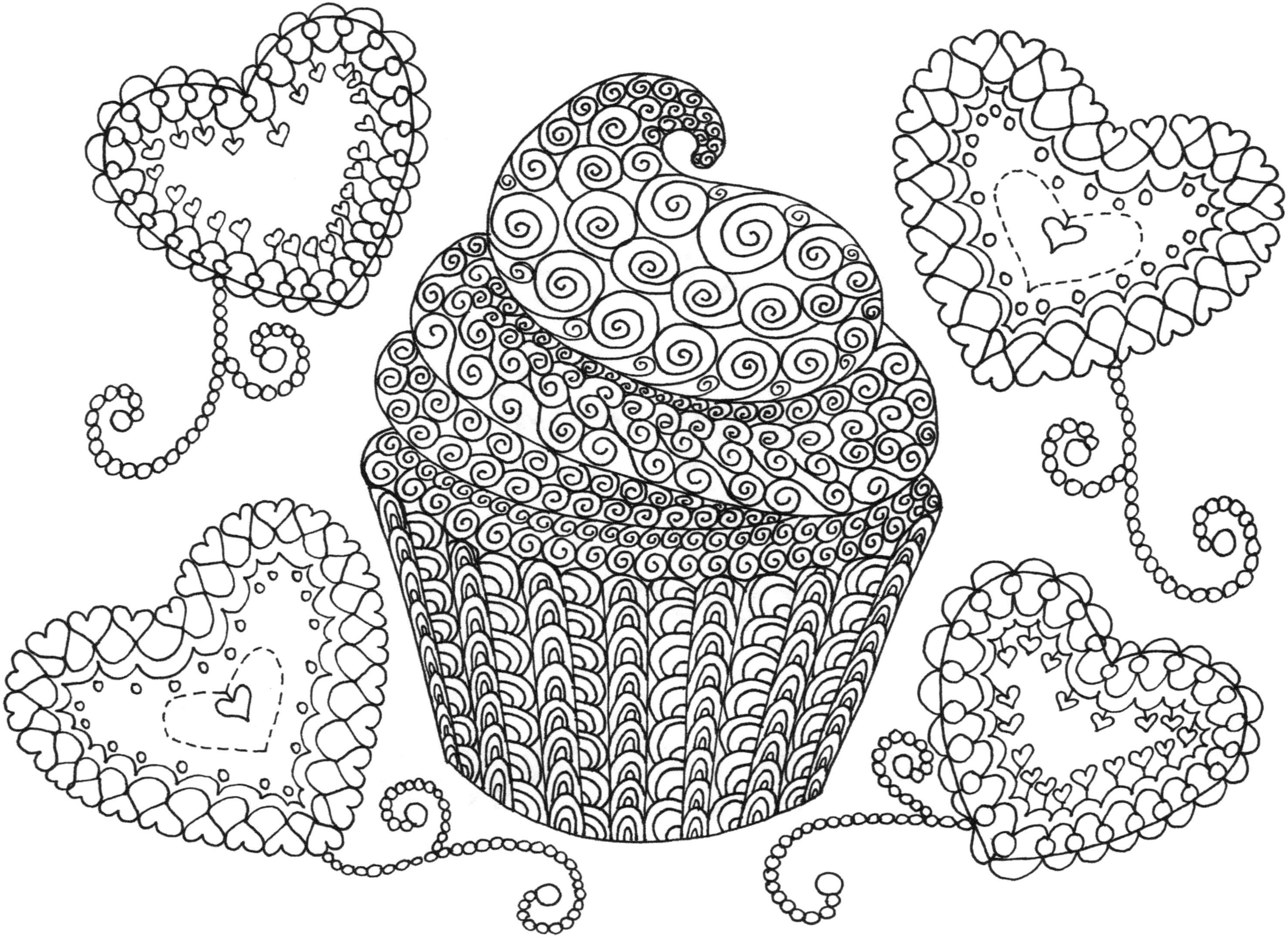

When you share

a cupcake,

you share

LOVE

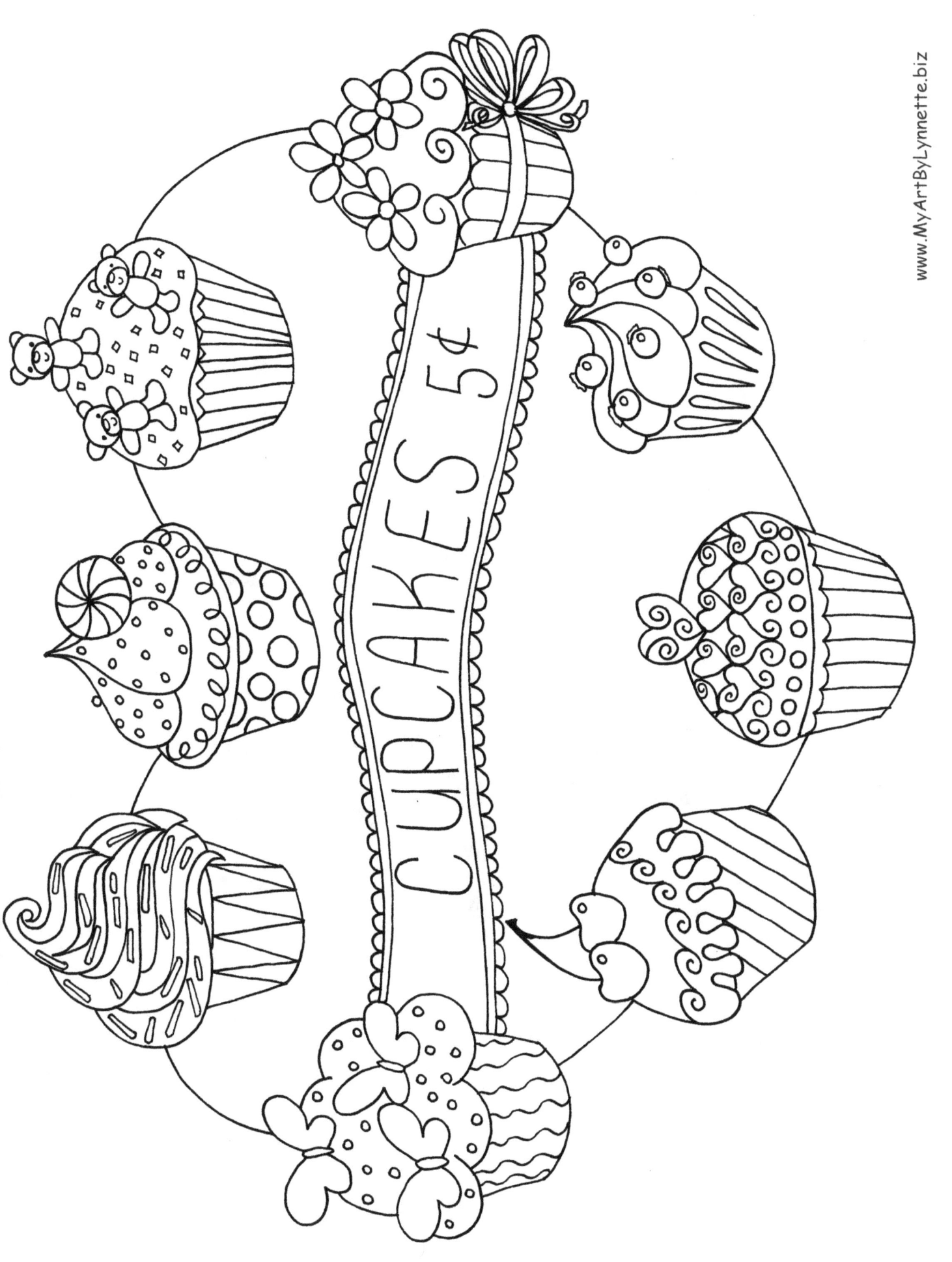

CUPCAKES 5¢

WHY YES,
A CUPCAKE
WITH SPRINKLES
WILL FIX
EVERYTHING

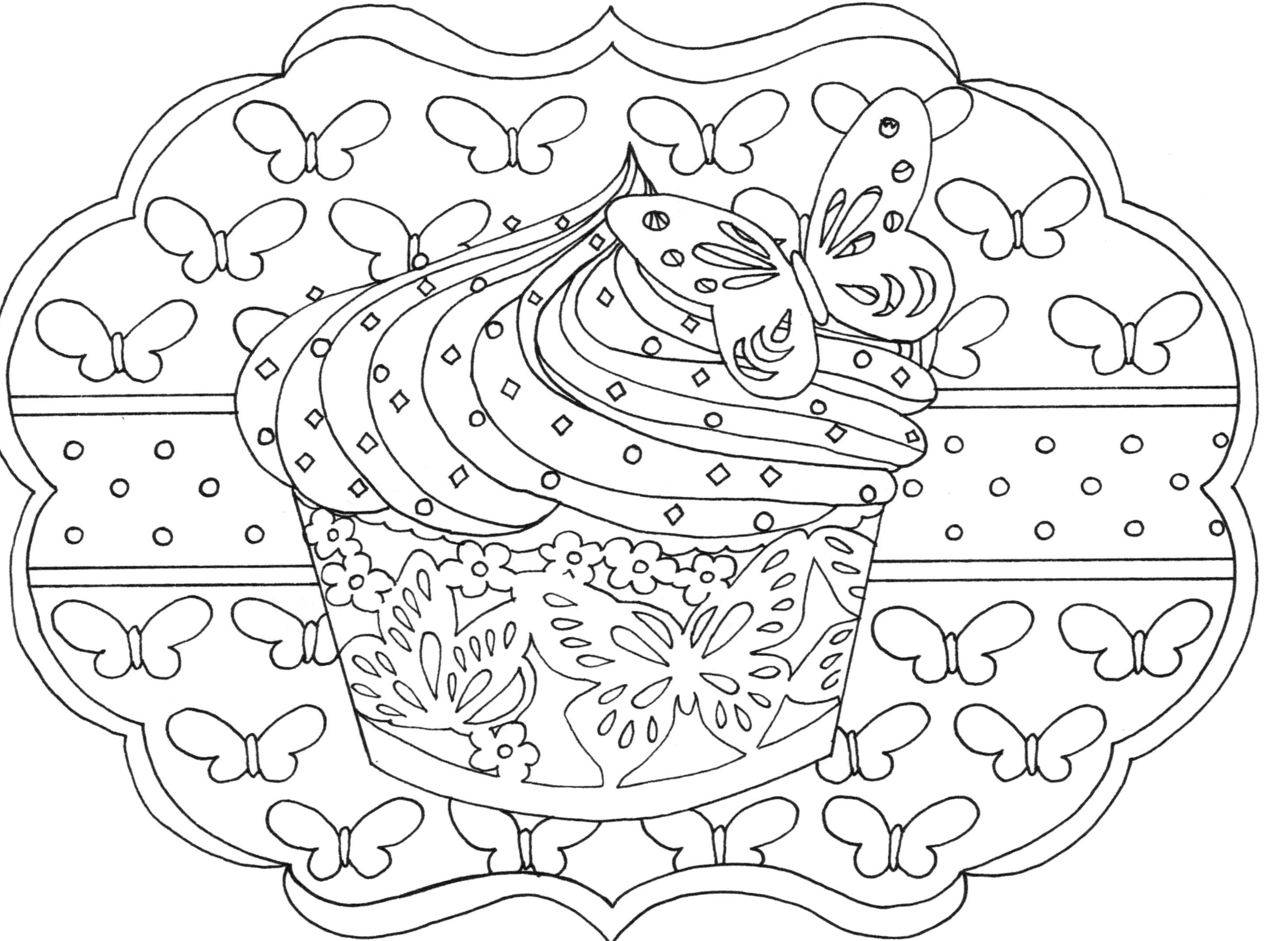

www.MyArtByLynnette.biz

Best Friends

don't let their BFF

eat the last

Cupcake

alone.

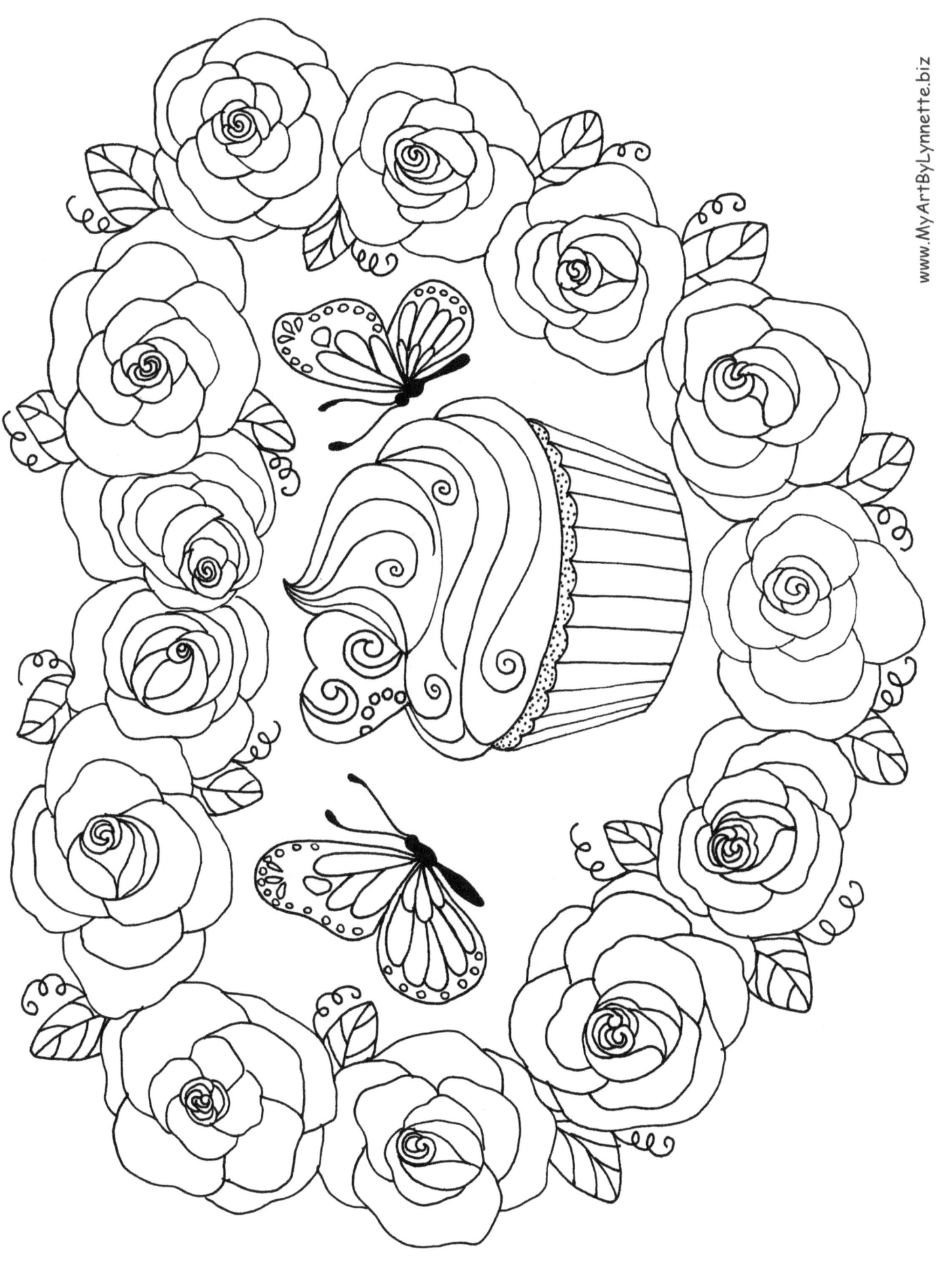

You are
the Strawberry
on top of
my Cupcake.

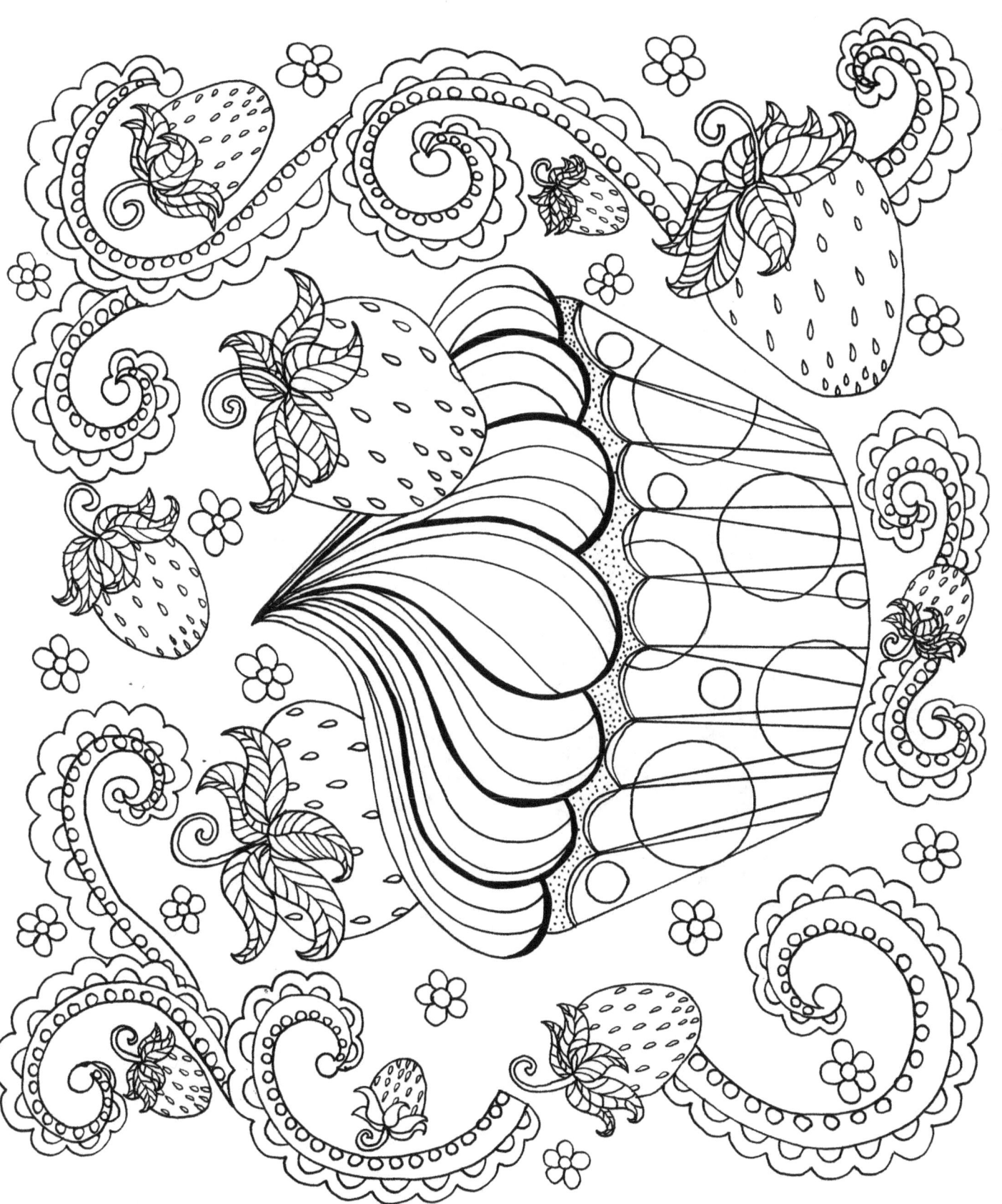

Happiness is...

sharing a

Cupcake with

you!

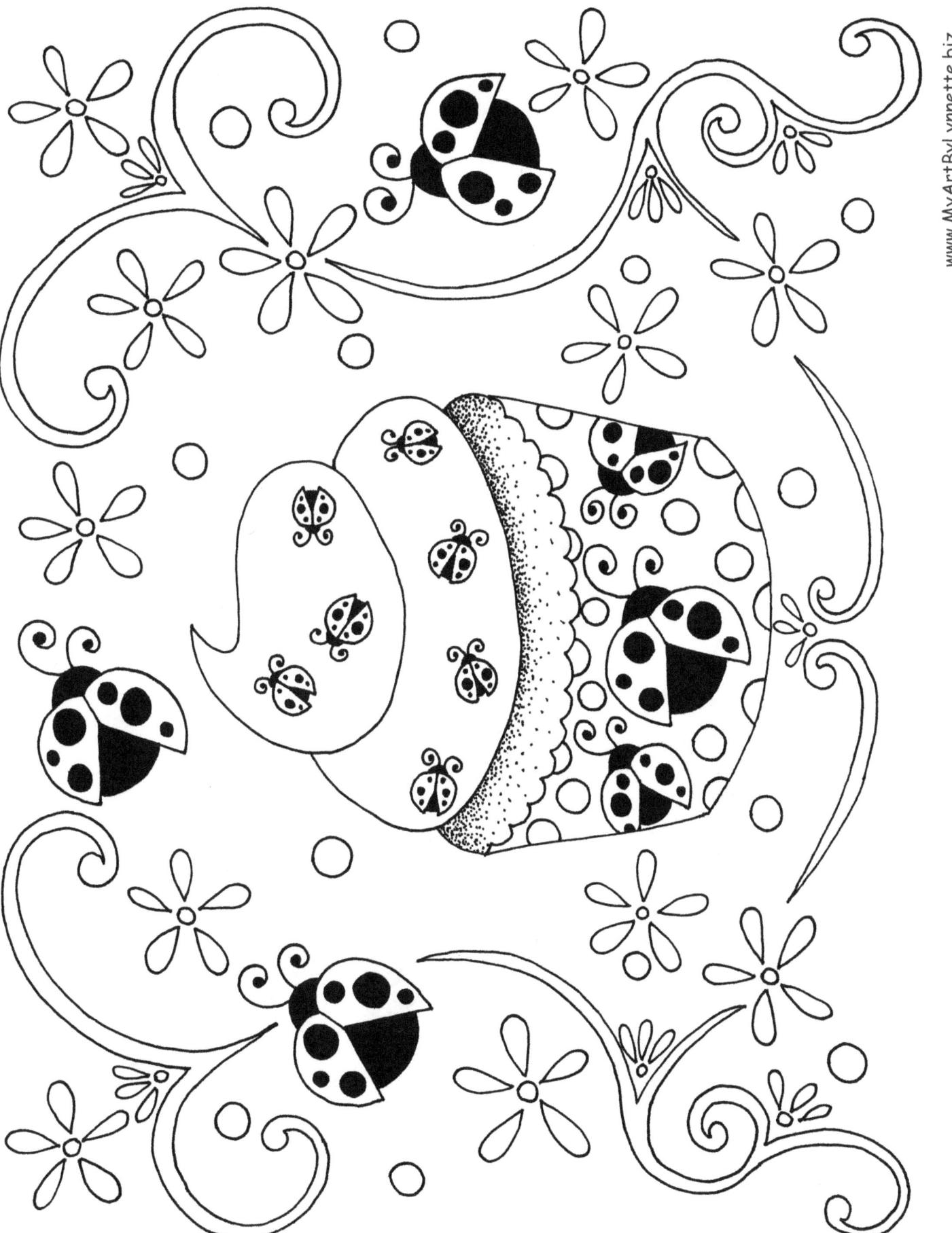

Take Life
as it comes,
and bake more
cupcakes.

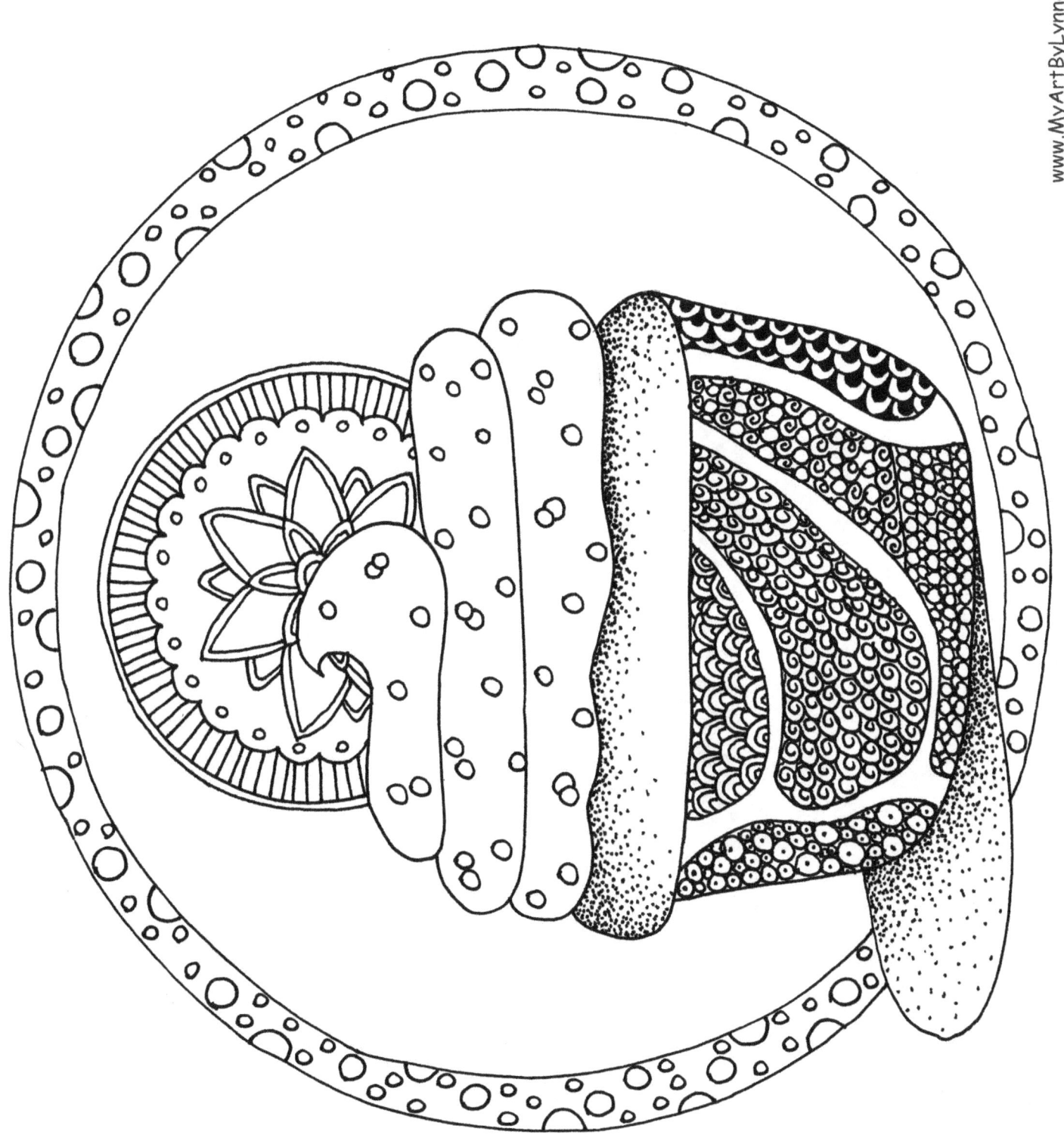

Happiness is...

Cupcakes with Sprinkes.

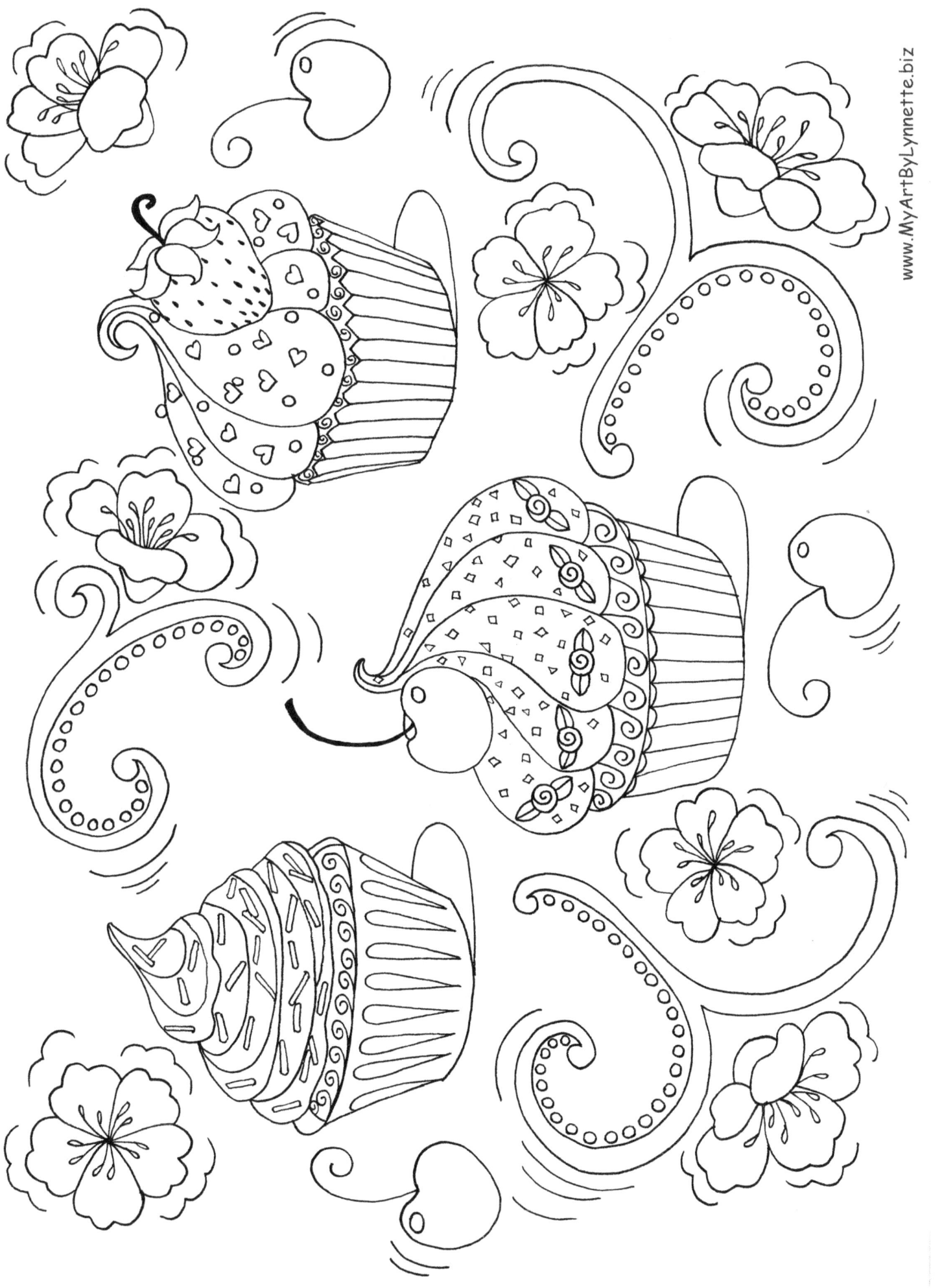

You have control over your actions alone

not over the fruits of your actions.

When we pay attention to the recipe

the cupcakes taste just right.

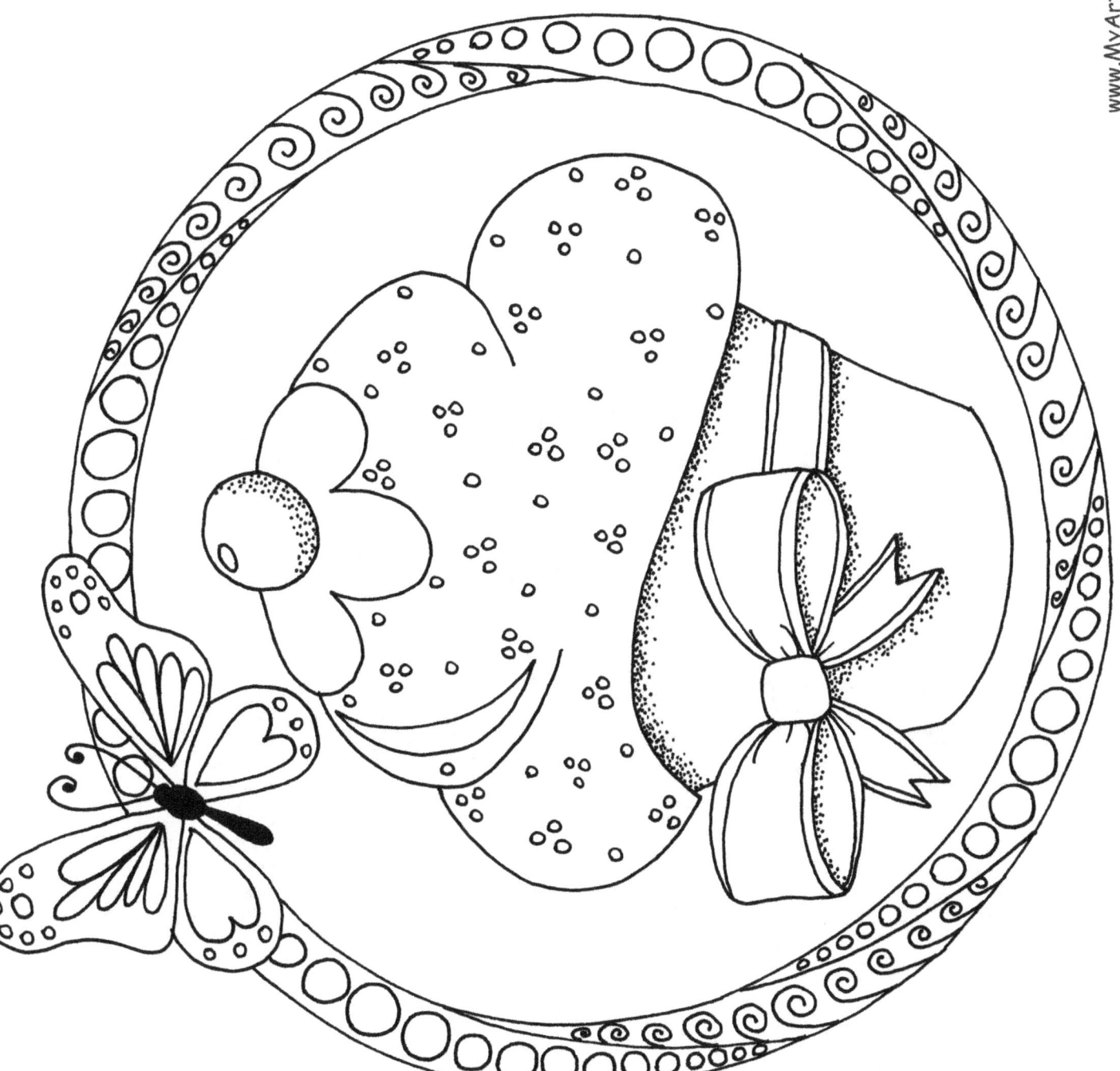

May the secret
ingredients of
Love and Happiness
flow from
your Heart and
into your mixing bowl.

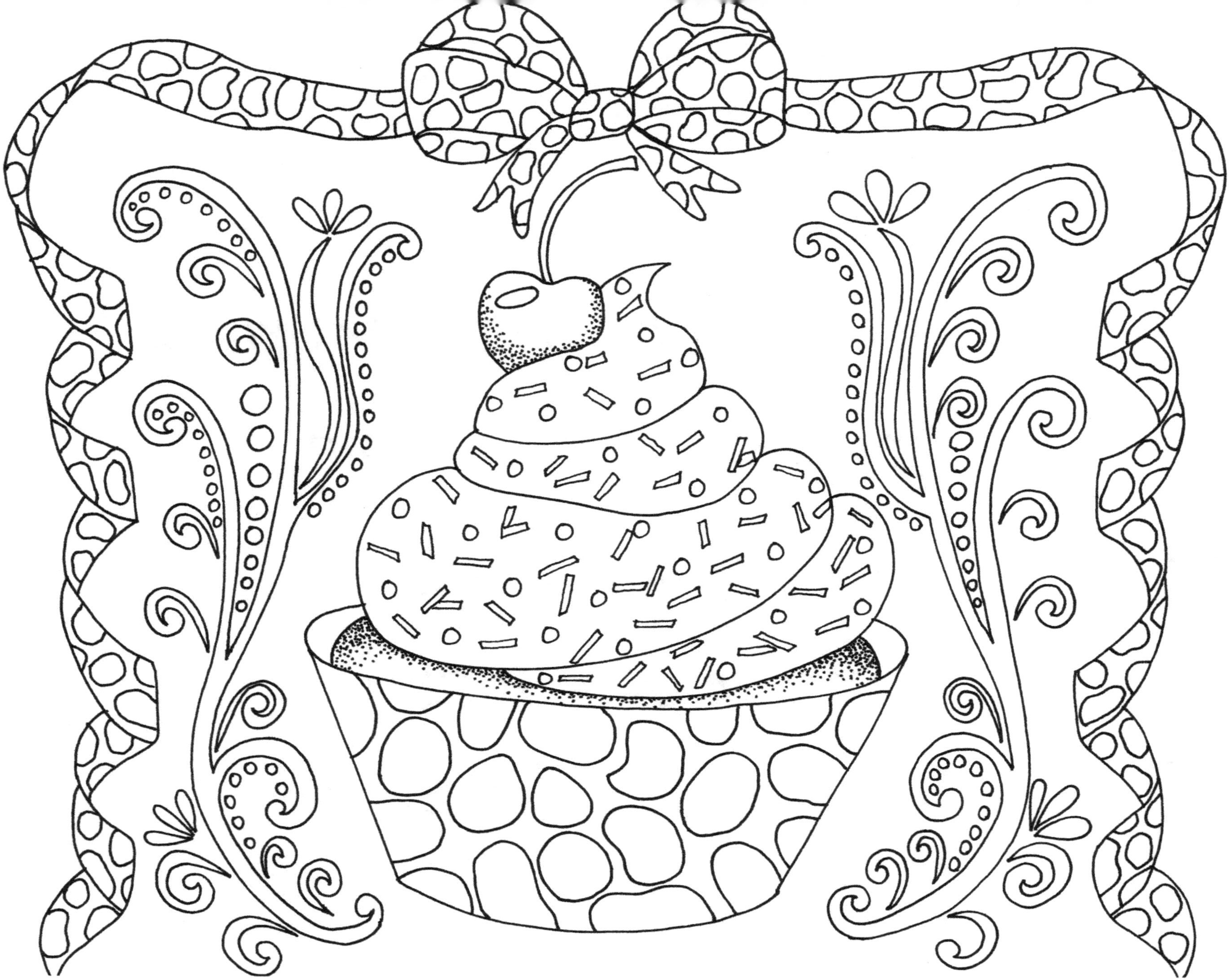

www.MyArtByLynnette.biz

Every Action

has a Reaction.

Teach a child to

bake cupcakes and

they will bake a better world.

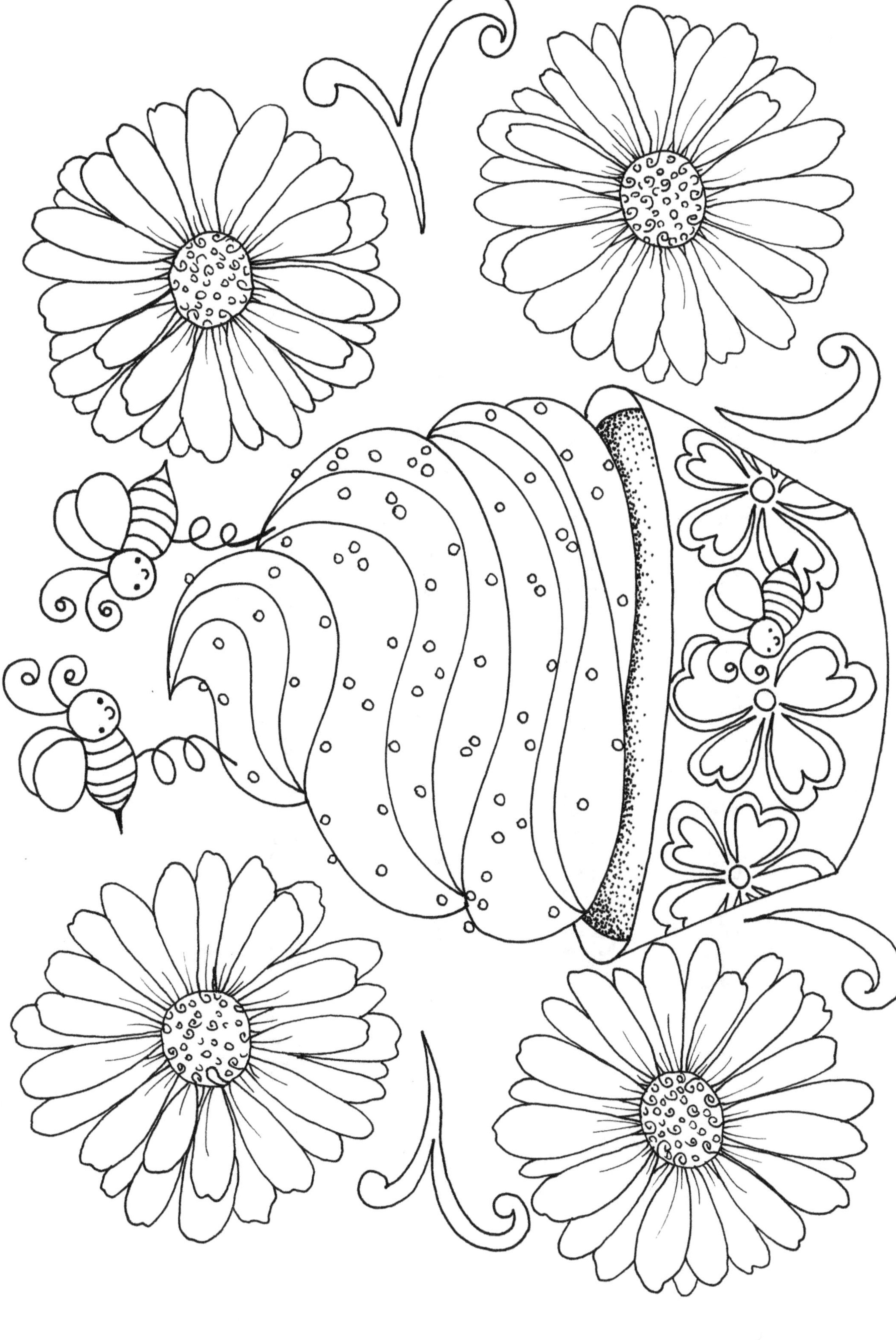

Hold onto the Highest

Never Compromise.

Pure, high quality ingredients make

the most delicious cupcakes.

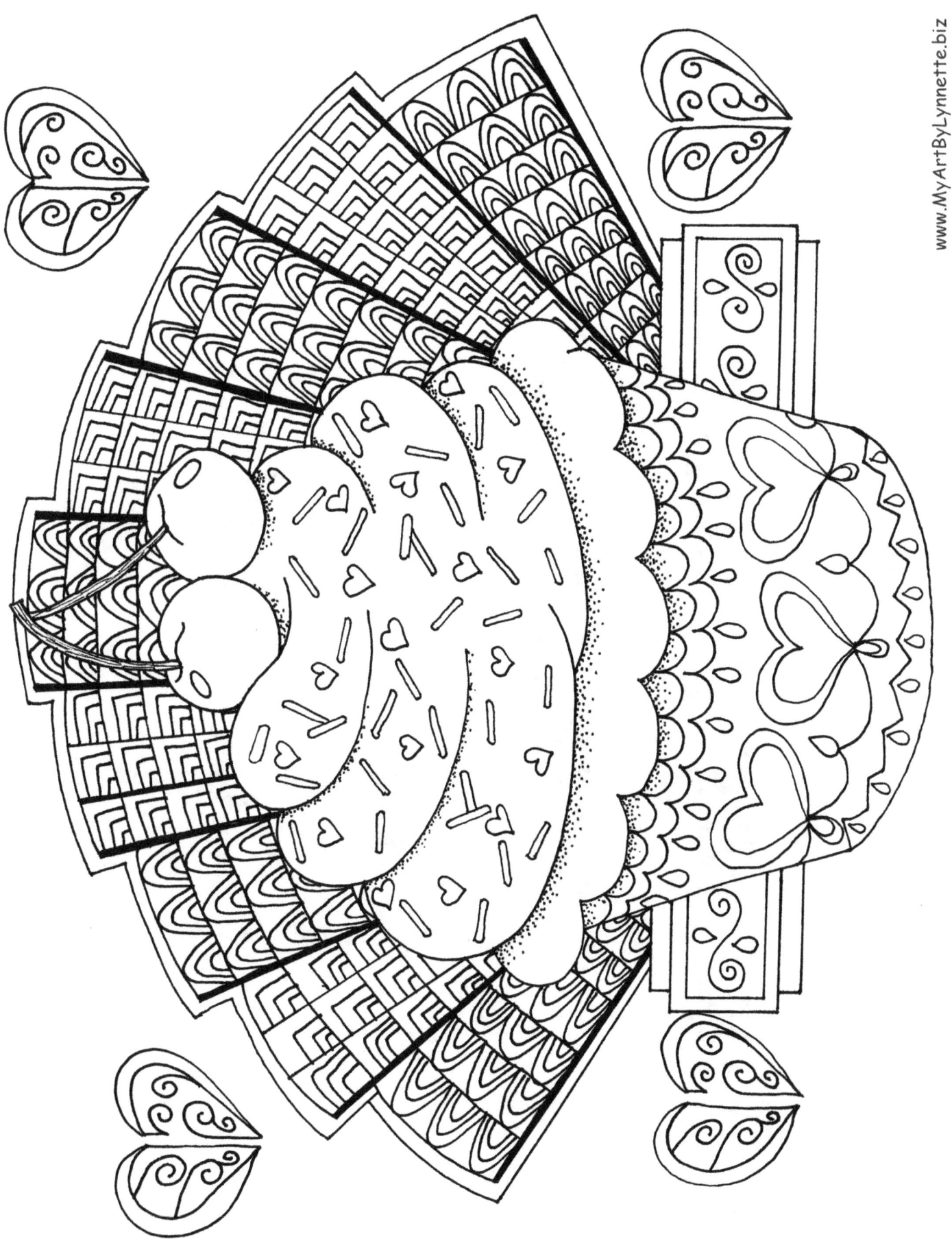

The whole cupcake is greater than the sum of the parts.

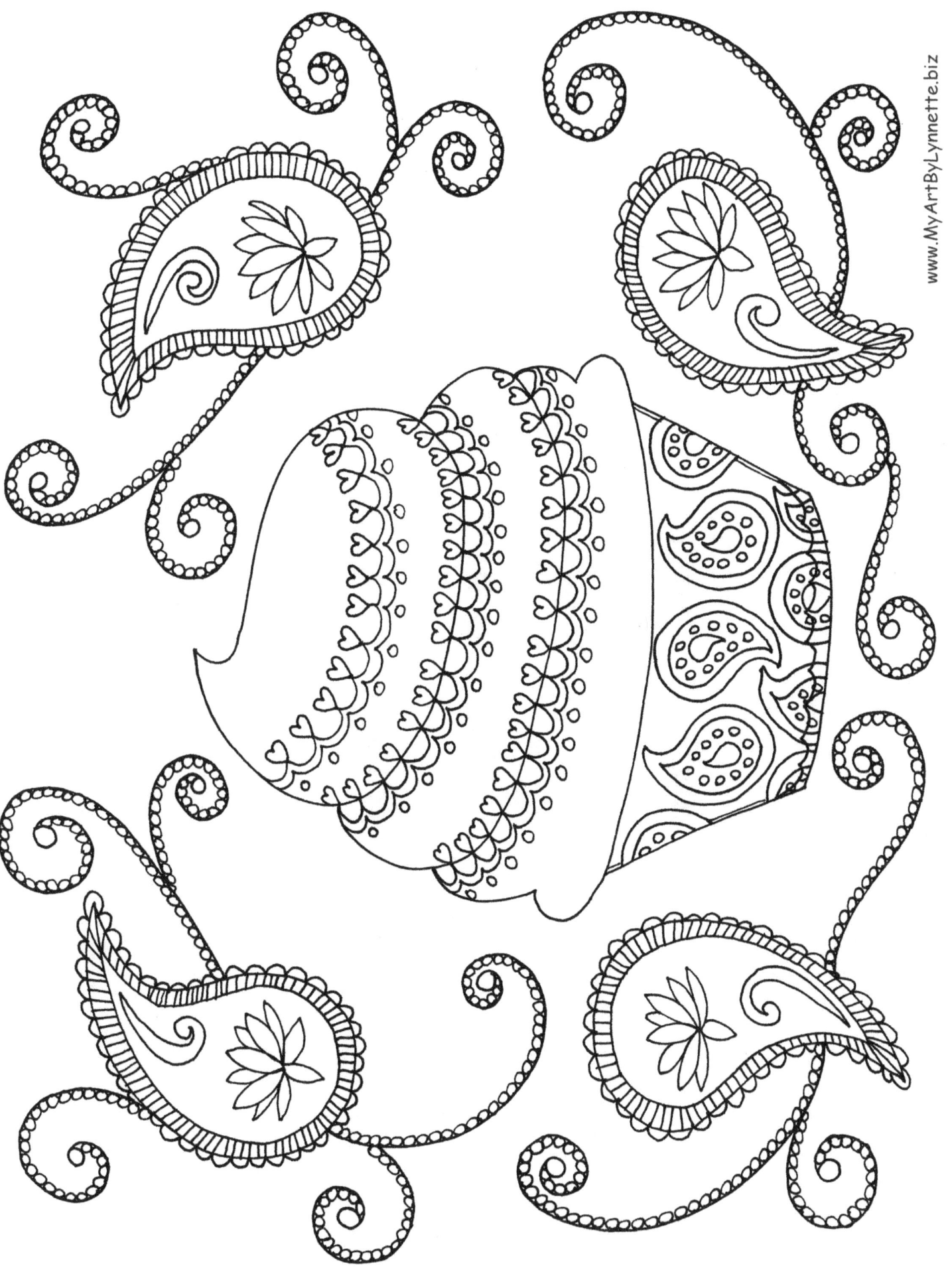

Seek the Highest

First.

You Deserve

the Best Cupcake in the Case.

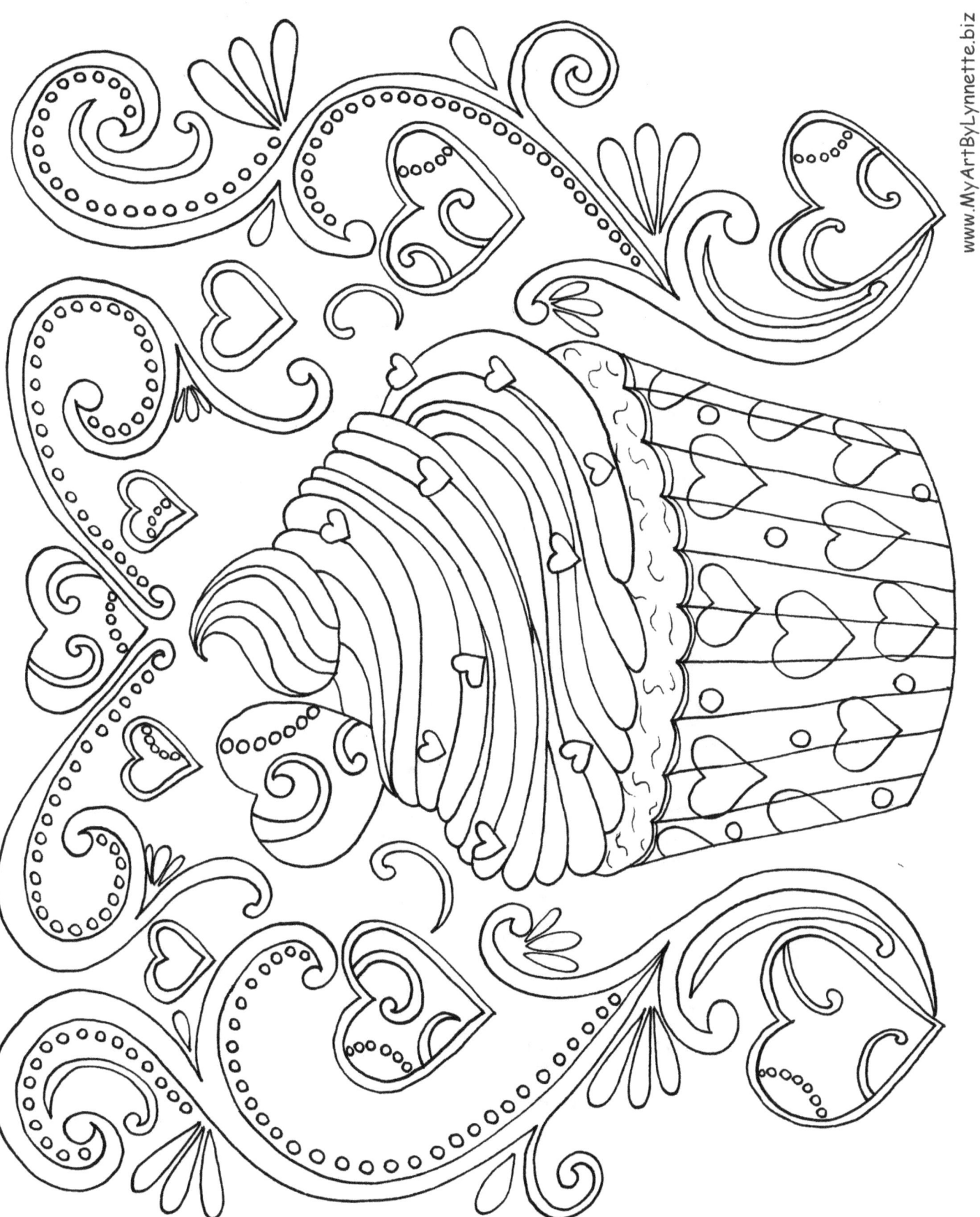

Thought leads to action.

May your cupcake desires always be fulfilled.

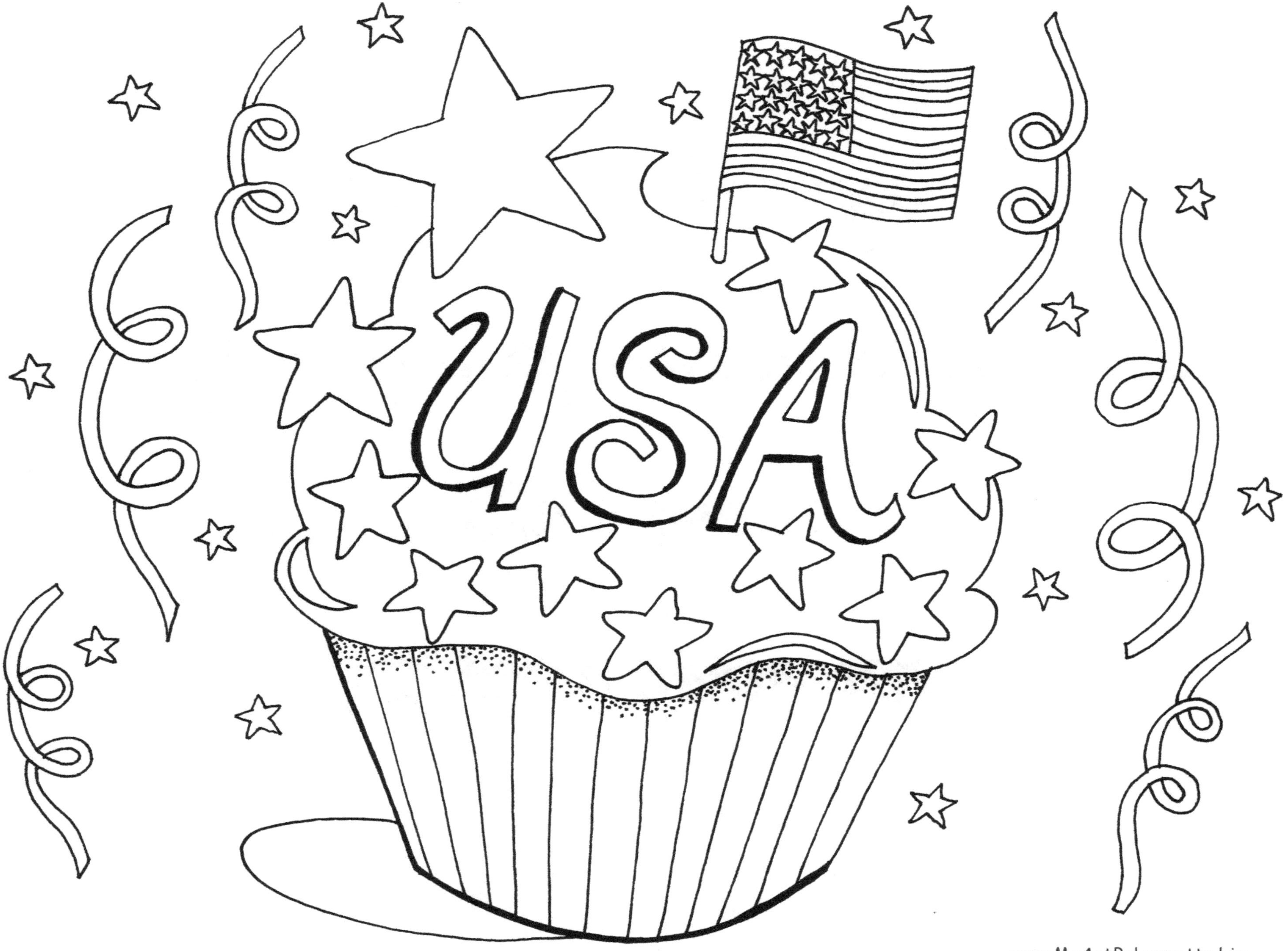

www.MyArtByLynnette.biz

Outer depends on inner.

You are the cream filling to my cupcake.

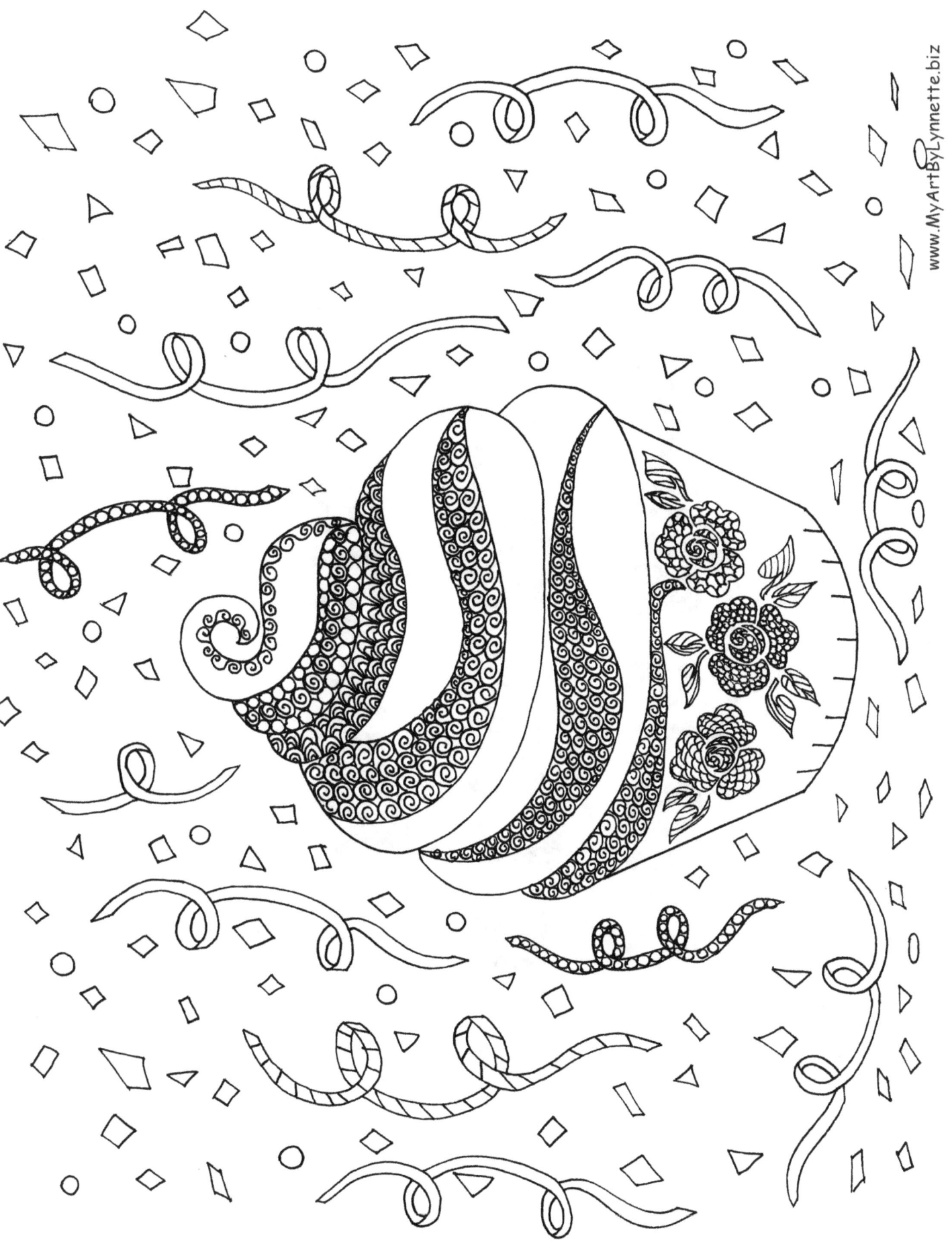

Life is sweet, but Cupcakes are Sweeter.

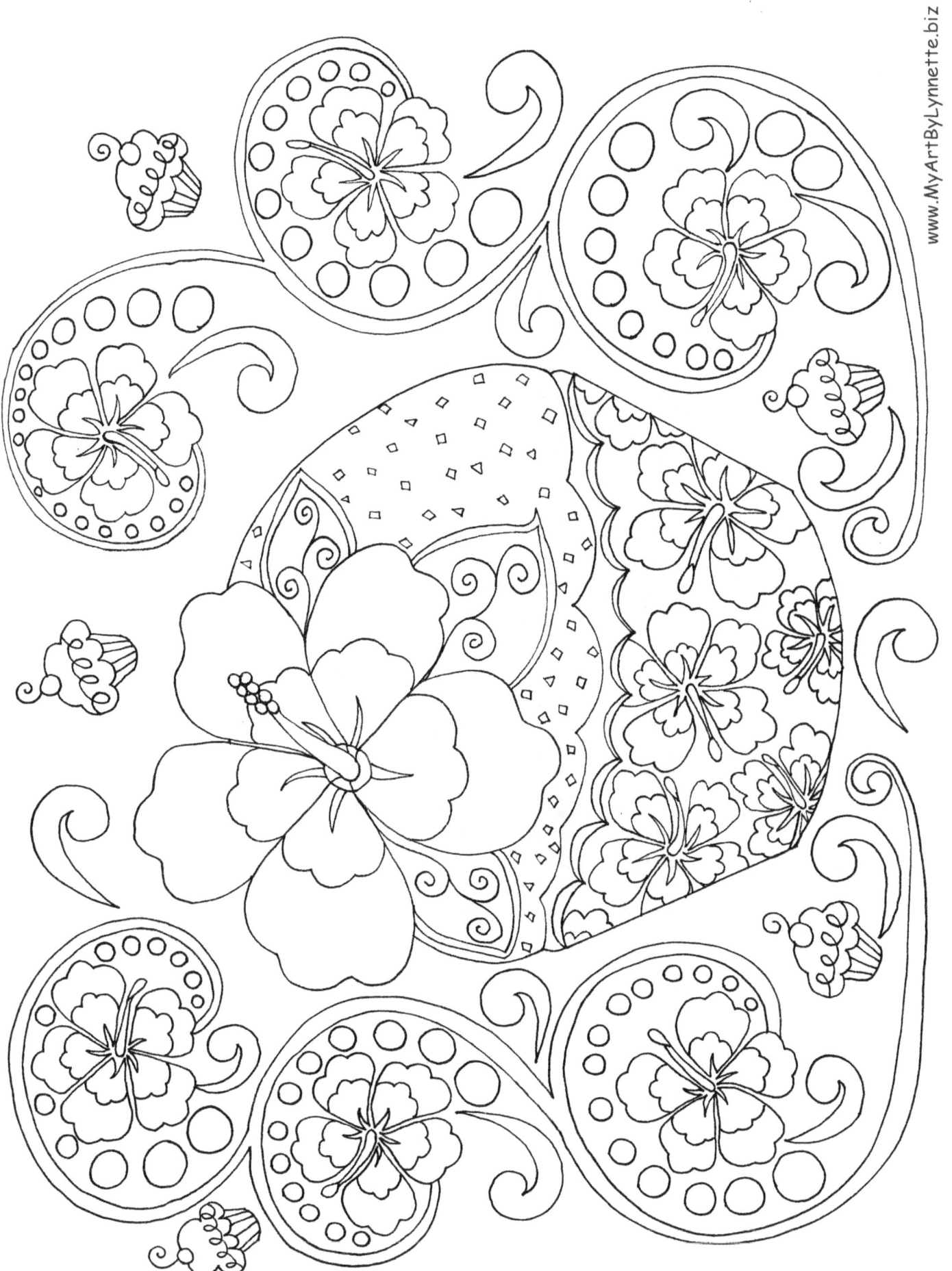

Harmony exists in Diversity.

Everyone gets along

when free Cupcakes

are served.

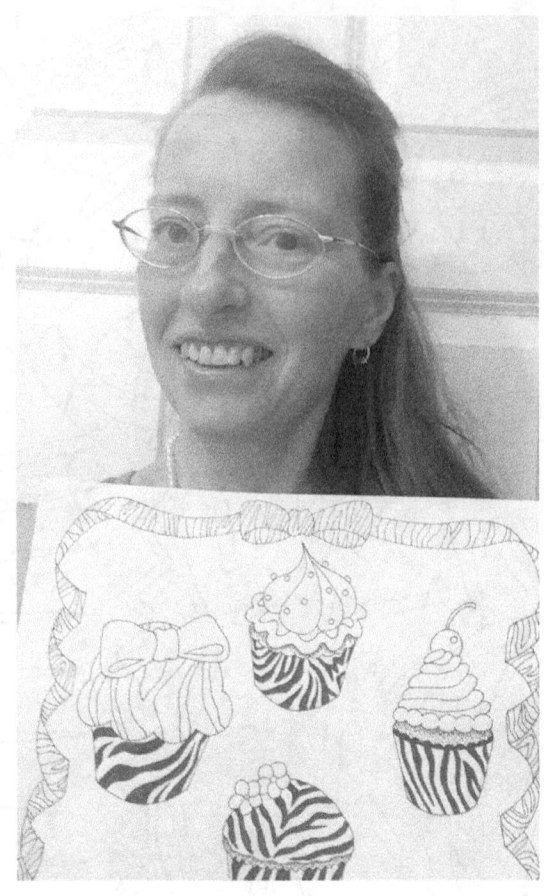

You can do anything you set your mind to. I set the goal of drawing one cupcake illustration a day. In one month, I had created all the cupcake drawings you see in this book. I hope you have many relaxing hours of stress free fun coloring my cupcake illustrations. My daughters and I plan to spend time together coloring all the cupcakes in this book. I am always amazed at all the cool color combinations that my daughters put together when we color together. Unleash your creativity and go wild with color on these cupcakes.

Please share your colored cupcake master pieces

email a photo to me at MyArtByLynnette@yahoo.com .

I will be sure to post your coloring photos on my blog on www.MyArtByLynnette.biz.

www.ingramcontent.com/pod-product-compliance
Lightning Source LLC
Chambersburg PA
CBHW080604190526
45169CB00007B/2873